When You Look Out the Window

How Phyllis Lyon and Del Martin Built a Community

by Gayle E. Pitman, PhD

illustrated by Christopher Lyles

MAGINATION PRESS • WASHINGTON, DC

American Psychological Association

To the tiny house at 651 Duncan Street—GP

To the hardest-working woman I know, my mother-in-law, Dr. Melinda Ramsby—CL

Published by
Magination Press ®
An Educational Publishing Foundation Book
American Psychological Association
750 First Street NE
Washington, DC 20002

Magination Press is a registered trademark of the American Psychological Association.

For more information about our books, including a complete catalog, please write to us, call 1-800-374-2721, or visit our website at www.apa.org/pubs/magination.

Book design by Susan White
Printed by Worzalla, Stevens Point, WI

Library of Congress Cataloging-in-Publication Data
Names: Pitman, Gayle E., author. | Lyles, Christopher, 1977– illustrator.
Title: When you look out the window : how Phyllis Lyon and Del Martin built a
    community / by Gayle E. Pitman, PhD ; illustrated by Christopher Lyles.
Description: Washington, DC : Magination Press, [2017] | Audience: Age 4–8.
    | "American Psychological Association."
Identifiers: LCCN 2016050777| ISBN 9781433827365 (hardcover)
    | ISBN 1433827360 (hardcover)
Subjects: LCSH: San Francisco (Calif.)—Description and travel—Juvenile literature. |
    Lyon, Phyllis—Juvenile literature. | Martin, Del—Juvenile literature.
    | Lesbian couples—California—San Francisco—Juvenile literature
Classification: LCC F869.S34 P58 2017 | DDC 979.4/61054—dc23 LC record available
    at https://lccn.loc.gov/2016050777

Manufactured in the United States of America
10 9 8 7 6 5 4 3 2 1

Many years ago, we met and became friends.

We fell in love.

We moved in together—on Valentine's Day!

We saved up all our money to buy this house.

And we sat, holding hands, and looked
out the window together.

We saw empty, quiet streets.

Doors tightly shut.

So many women
who didn't have rights.

People who were afraid of us.

People who didn't think we should love each other.

No feeling of community.

So we worked to change that.

When you look out the window now, what do you see?

There is a beautiful red bridge.

And there's a rainbow at the end of the tunnel.

The rainbow tunnel's been here as long as we have.

There is a church with a bell tower
that reaches for the sky.

The doors are wide open.

The streets are filled
with people waiting to get in.

Over there is the most colorful building ever.

There are women's faces painted all over it, and they're looking right back at you!

They look strong and powerful.

Over by the water, you'll see a building with a garden on top. That one! The one with pine trees and waterfalls.

And a row of colored flags in front of it.

You'll see a building that looks REALLY important.

It has a big dome with a shiny golden top.

At night, in the summertime, the front lights up like a rainbow.

Look just down the road, over there.
You'll see a building that's made out of windows.

It looks like it's warm in there.

Our names are on the building next to it.

That is a very warm place too.

At the bottom of our street, you'll see the biggest rainbow flag in the world, flapping in the wind.

And if you squint REALLY hard, right next to that you'll see two little outfits displayed in a window. They look like doll clothes from here! One is purple, and the other is blue.

Those are our favorite colors.

So today,
we don't see
what we saw,
so long ago.

We see busy streets filled with friendly people.

We see open doors.

We see women who can do ANYTHING!

We see pretty flowers and trees.

We see love.

We see a big rainbow community!

Reading Guide

Phyllis Lyon and Del Martin were one of San Francisco's most well-known and politically active lesbian couples. They met in 1950, and moved in together on February 14, 1953 (Valentine's Day!). The house they shared for 53 years—and where Phyllis still lives today—located at the top of Castro Street, has a big picture window that overlooks the entire city. Each of the landmarks described in the story is part of the view from their house. Phyllis and Del left their mark on each of these sites, and they are described below.

"There is a beautiful red bridge. And there's a rainbow at the end of the tunnel."

The Golden Gate Bridge is one of the most recognizable and iconic structures in the world. It was featured on the program cover for the first annual Daughters of Bilitis (DOB) national convention in 1960, held at the Hotel Whitcomb in downtown San Francisco. In 1953, when Phyllis and Del moved to San Francisco, they had a very hard time meeting other lesbians. At that time, most lesbians and gay men were deeply in the closet, and being out and visible meant risking being fired from one's job, arrested and jailed, or institutionalized and treated for the "disorder" of homosexuality. In 1955, Phyllis and Del, along with six other women, founded the DOB as a way to create a safe, private social space for lesbians. It quickly became focused on political issues as well, and was the first lesbian rights organization in the United States. A year later, in 1956, Phyllis became the first editor of *The Ladder*, the DOB's official publication. *The Ladder* offered an opportunity for lesbians who lived far from an active DOB chapter to connect with other lesbians and learn about lesbian politics and culture. *The Ladder* helped the organization to grow, and by 1959, DOB chapters had been established throughout the United States.

"There is a church with a bell tower that reaches for the sky."

Phyllis worked for many years at Glide Urban Center, a program affiliated with Glide Memorial Church in the Tenderloin district. At the time, people who were gay or lesbian were condemned by religion and were not welcome in many churches. In 1964, three pastors—Ted McIlvenna, Cecil Williams, and Don Kuhn—formed the Council on Religion and the Homosexual, which worked to create acceptance for gay and lesbian people within the churches. Phyllis and Del joined this organization shortly after it was formed, and both served on the board of directors. Their first book, *Lesbian/Woman*, was published by Glide Publications and is now considered to be a classic.

"Over there is the most colorful building ever."

The Women's Building is a feminist and social justice–oriented community space located in the heart of the Mission District. Much of Phyllis and Del's activism revolved around feminism and women's rights. One of the major goals of the feminist movement was to establish public spaces specifically for women, and the Women's Building in San Francisco was one example of that. The first Women's Building was established in 1893 in Chicago as an exhibit at the World's Columbian Exposition. Designed by architect Sophia Hayden, the Women's Building featured women's accomplishments in the arts, literature, and culture. Decades later, in the 1970s, more Women's Buildings were established, this time with a much more political focus. The first, the Woman's Building in Los Angeles (named after the Chicago Women's Building), was founded in 1973. Later, in 1979, the San Francisco Women's Centers (co-founded by Del Martin) purchased the Women's Building in the Mission District.

Many feminist groups, including the National Organization for Women (NOW), held meetings in these Women's Buildings. NOW was founded in 1966, and Phyllis and Del joined the following year. Back then, the presence of lesbians in the women's movement was considered to be "the lavender menace," and lesbians were not openly welcomed into the movement. By 1971, largely due to Phyllis and Del's efforts, NOW began to include lesbian rights in their political agenda. Later, Del was the first out lesbian to be elected to NOW's board of directors. Del's activism also focused on violence against women. Her book *Battered Wives* was one of the first to attribute domestic violence to institutionalized sexism. Del co-founded the Coalition for Justice for Battered Women in 1975, La Casa de las Madres (a shelter for battered women) in 1976, and the California Coalition Against Domestic Violence in 1977.

"Over by the water, you'll see a building with a garden on top."

The Moscone Convention Center is named after former mayor George Moscone, a heterosexual man who was a strong advocate for gay and lesbian people. Moscone worked closely with San Francisco Board of Supervisors member Harvey Milk, the first openly gay person to be elected to public office in California. The south block of Yerba Buena Gardens sits atop the Moscone Center. Phyllis and Del helped form the Alice B. Toklas Democratic Club, which campaigned for candidates who supported gay rights. In 1976, Moscone appointed Del to the San Francisco Human Rights Commission, and later asked her to chair the San Francisco Commission on the Status of Women. Two years later, in 1978, Phyllis became the chair of a group called San Franciscans Against Proposition 6 (also known as the "Briggs Initiative"). Had it passed, teachers in K–12 public schools could have been fired just for being gay or lesbian. With the support of many other allies, Proposition 6 was struck down. Despite that victory, that year came to a tragic end; on November 27, 1978, both Moscone and Milk were assassinated.

"You'll see a building that looks REALLY important. It has a big dome with a shiny golden top."

San Francisco City Hall is the center of the city's local government. It is also where Phyllis and Del were legally married—twice! On February 12, 2004, just over 50 years after moving to San Francisco, Phyllis and Del were married at City Hall after then-mayor Gavin Newsom ordered that marriage licenses should be granted to same-sex couples if they requested them. Their marriage license was voided on August 14, 2004. On June 16, 2008, they were married once again by Gavin Newsom when the California Supreme Court ruled that same-sex marriage was legal. This was Del's last political act before her death on August 27, 2008. Later that year, California voters passed Proposition 8, which outlawed same-sex marriages. After that, other states began to enact bans on same-sex marriage. As a result, many people throughout the United States joined the marriage equality movement. By 2012, President Obama made a public statement in support of same-sex marriage, and in 2015, the Supreme Court ruled that marriage is a fundamental right for same-sex couples.

"You'll see a building that's made out of windows."

The San Francisco LGBT Community Center, with its "wall of windows," opened its solar-powered facility at 1800 Market Street in 2002. Less than a block away is Lyon-Martin Health Services, named in honor of Phyllis and Del. Lyon-Martin Health Services was established in 1978, the same year Harvey Milk was assassinated. At that time, the women's health movement was a strong force in the feminist movement, with organizations like Planned Parenthood leading the charge. However, not all of these clinics were knowledgeable about lesbian health. Very few doctors knew anything about the challenges lesbians faced in the health care system, and women often didn't have a say in their own health care. A group of medical practitioners decided to take action, and they put together a pilot study on lesbian health. The researchers learned that many lesbians didn't access health care because of homophobia and sexism, and so they decided to establish a health service that was more welcoming and inclusive. Because of Phyllis and Del's activism, the founders decided they wanted to name the health clinic after them. Lyon-Martin Health Services was an integral part of the women's health movement, and continues to be at the forefront of health care for people who are lesbian, gay, bisexual, transgender, and/or queer (LGBTQ). Today, largely as a result of this movement, there are a wide range of health centers designated specifically for lesbians. Some, like the Lesbian Health Initiative in Houston, Texas, are stand-alone clinics; others, such as Lesbian Health Services in Denver, Colorado, and the LGBTQ Clinic in Coralville, Iowa, are part of larger health care organizations.

"At the bottom of our street, you'll see the biggest rainbow flag in the world, flapping in the wind."

The Castro District is one of the most well-known LGBTQ neighborhoods in the world. Its gay male population began to grow after World War II, and by the late 1960s, it had earned a reputation for being a gay mecca. Because it was generally unsafe for LGBTQ people to be out, they began creating their own safe neighborhood spaces. Some were in large urban areas, such as Greenwich Village in New York City, Washington Square West in Philadelphia, and Boystown in Chicago. Others were in more outlying areas, such as Northampton, Massachusetts; Palm Springs, California; Asheville, North Carolina; and Provincetown, Massachusetts. In San Francisco, a huge rainbow flag flies at the corner of Market and Castro Streets. A block away from the rainbow flag is the GLBT History Museum, which opened their doors to the public in December of 2010. The GLBT Historical Society, which oversees the museum, houses many of Phyllis and Del's papers. The museum also displays the purple and blue pantsuits Phyllis and Del wore when they got married—both times.

Note to Parents, Caregivers, and Educators

People who are lesbian, gay, bisexual, transgender, and/or queer (LGBTQ) are more visible and accepted in our society than ever before. However, anyone who wants to learn about LGBTQ history and culture will probably have to search for that information on their own. Many students have never learned anything about LGBTQ history. They may not have realized that some of the authors whose works they read (or whose works were read to them) were LGBTQ. They may not know that major discoveries and contributions to the fields of science, mathematics, and technology were made by LGBTQ people. And they may not be aware of the ways in which LGBTQ people have been oppressed, and what they did to fight back against it.

In a now-classic article titled "Mirrors, Windows, and Sliding Glass Doors," Rudine Sims Bishop said:

Books are sometimes windows, offering views of worlds that may be real or imagined, familiar or strange. These windows are also sliding glass doors, and readers have only to walk through in imagination to become part of whatever world has been created or recreated by the author. When lighting conditions are just right, however, a window can also be a mirror. Literature transforms human experience and reflects it back to us, and in that reflection we can see our own lives and experiences as part of the larger human experience. Reading, then, becomes a means of self-affirmation, and readers often seek their mirrors in books.

Essentially, children look for images of themselves in the books they read. And many children, particularly White children from heterosexual families, find them. Unfortunately, many do not. Children from historically marginalized groups don't always see positive and empowering images of themselves in books or other forms of media, and their histories aren't always well represented in school materials. LGBTQ history and culture, in particular, is routinely erased or omitted entirely from school curricula, often resulting in a complete absence of LGBTQ-related information. When children can't find reflections of themselves and their families in books or other materials—or if those reflections are inaccurate or distorted—that sends a powerfully negative message to them. It tells them that they don't exist, that they don't matter, or that there's something wrong with them or unnatural about them. That's why books like *When You Look Out the Window* are so important—because they share histories of people whose stories don't always get told.

Why Is It Important to Teach Children LGBTQ History and Culture?

Exposing children to culturally-rich learning materials is vitally important, for a variety of reasons:

- **It can boost self-esteem.**

  Seeing oneself reflected in books, TV, movies, and learning materials helps to nurture a sense of pride in children. It helps them learn who they are and where they came from. Knowing our history is a fundamental building block of identity development. Moreover, when children can identify with people who have made great accomplishments (like Phyllis and Del have), that can foster a sense of pride in them.

- **It helps to prevent and counteract stereotypes.**

  Children can form stereotypes about people as early as preschool. Those stereotypes often form in the absence of accurate and meaningful information. Lesbian women, for example, are very underrepresented in nonfiction books for children, and the absence of their stories can contribute to the development of stereotypes. In contrast, when books and other learning materials provide good-quality information about a wide range of people, children can develop a more robust understanding of them.

- **It can promote empathy.**

  Schools are places where children can explore new and unfamiliar things. When children engage in meaningful learning opportunities about people who are different from them, they are more likely to develop a sense of empathy and kindness towards them.

- **It can help children become more socially aware.**

  Part of learning about any historically marginalized group, including LGBTQ people, involves discussing the issue of prejudice and discrimination. When Phyllis and Del first moved to San Francisco in the 1950s, they didn't feel welcomed, because at that time most people believed that it was unhealthy and unnatural for two women to love each other.

- **It can help prevent bullying and harassment.**

  LGBTQ youth are often the targets of teasing, bullying, verbal harassment, and physical violence. Many believe that this kind of bullying is more likely to occur in schools where there is a negative climate for LGBTQ students—and the omission of LGBTQ content from school curricula contributes to that climate. Infusing the curriculum with

LGBTQ-themed material communicates a culture of visibility, respect, and acceptance to students.

- **It helps children develop perspective-taking skills.**
  For children who come from LGBTQ families (or who are LGBTQ-identified), books like *When You Look Out the Window* serve as mirrors for them. For other children, they provide a window into another set of experiences. When children are exposed to stories about people who are different from them, it helps them develop the ability to step out of their own personal frame of reference, and view the world through a different lens.

- **When culturally-rich content is infused across disciplines, it gives all children the opportunity to visualize themselves in a wider range of careers.**
  Being LGBTQ is invisible to most people. Unless someone publicly comes out, it's impossible to know for sure whether someone is lesbian, gay, bisexual, or transgender. Because of that, even though many great writers, artists, mathematicians, scientists, and political figures have been LGBTQ-identified, most children don't learn about that. Making this aspect of their identities visible helps children see LGBTQ people as contributors to our history and culture, and as potential role models for themselves.

How Can You Use This Book With Children?

If you are a parent, you can use this book as an opportunity to share a slice of LGBTQ history with your child. Your child may ask questions as you read the book (such as "Why were people afraid of them?"), and this is a great opportunity to talk to your child about issues LGBTQ people often face.

If you are a librarian, you can use this book as part of a display for LGBTQ History Month (which occurs every October) and/or LGBTQ Pride Month (which takes place in June). This helps foster LGBTQ visibility for library users. You can also develop programming that features LGBTQ historical figures.

If you are a teacher, you can play a special role in the effort to increase LGBTQ visibility for children. Many children who are from historically marginalized groups lack meaningful and accurate reflections of themselves. That said, when parents share the same culture as their children, they often pass their history and their culture down to them. Food, language, clothing, celebrations and traditions, and stories are often shared within families. LGBTQ people, however, don't usually have families who pass history and culture down to them. This is where schools can play an important role in filling that gap. Finding ways to include LGBTQ-related content into your curriculum is a powerful way of keeping LGBTQ history, culture, and contributions to society alive.

Additional Resources

The FAIR Education Act website was created as a resource for teachers in California public schools. SB 48 (also known as the FAIR Education Act) requires that schools include fair, accurate, inclusive, and respectful representations of people with disabilities and LGBTQ people in history and social studies curriculum at all grade levels. Although this resource is based in California, it is useful for educators across the United States: http://www.faireducationact.com

The Gay, Lesbian, & Straight Education Network (GLSEN) offers LGBTQ-inclusive lesson plans that are aligned with Common Core standards: http://www.glsen.org/educate/resources/curriculum

The Genders & Sexualities Alliance Network (GSA Network) is an organization targeting older students (middle school and high school). However, they provide information that can be useful for teachers, librarians, and parents. They have resources for learning about LGBTQ Black history: https://gsanetwork.org/BlackedOUTHistory And resources for learning about LGBTQ Latinx history: https://gsanetwork.org/nuestroarcoiris

The GLBT Historical Society offers a wealth of information to the general public about LGBTQ history. They operate the GLBT History Museum in San Francisco, and they also oversee a wide range of archival collections, many of which can be accessed online: http://www.glbthistory.org

About the Author

Gayle E. Pitman, PhD, is a professor of psychology and women's studies at Sacramento City College. Her teaching and writing focuses on gender and sexual orientation, and she has worked extensively with the lesbian, gay, bisexual, transgender, and queer (LGBTQ) community. She is the author of *This Day In June*, which won the 2015 Stonewall Book Award—Mike Morgan and Larry Romans Children's and Young Adult Literature Award.

About the Illustrator

Christopher Lyles has illustrated numerous books for children. Inspired by vintage graphics and antique surfaces, he uses collage and mixed media applications to create his art. He lives in a quiet New England town surrounded by wilderness. When he is not creating picture books, he enjoys spending time with his family and hiking the surrounding woods. The illustrations for *When You Look Out the Window* were created using watercolor, collage, and mixed media.

About Magination Press

Magination Press is an imprint of the American Psychological Association, the largest scientific and professional organization representing psychologists in the United States and the largest association of psychologists worldwide.